A WORLD AFTER . . .

SUPER-PLAGUE

Anne Rooney

Chicago, Illinois

To contact Capstone Global Library, please call 800-747-4992, or visit our web site www.capstonepub.com

Edited by Andrew Farrow, Adrian Vigliano, and Vaarunika Dharmapala
Designed by Philippa Jenkins
Original illustrations © Capstone Global Library Limited 2013
Illustrated by HL Studios and Alvaro Fernandez Villa Advocate-Art pp4-5
Picture research by Mica Brancic
Printed in the United States of America in North Mankato, Minnesota.
122013 007920RP

We would like to thank David Wright for his invaluable help in the preparation of this book.

Library of Congress Cataloging-in-Publication Data

Rooney, Anne.
  Super-plague / Anne Rooney.
    pages cm.—(A world after)
  Includes bibliographical references and index.
  ISBN 978-1-4329-7621-7 (hb)—ISBN 978-1-4329-7626-2 (pb) 1. Emerging infectious diseases. 2. World health—Forecasting. 3. Epidemics—Prevention. I. Title.

  RA643.R68 2014
  362.1969—dc23   2012035017

Acknowledgments

We would like to thank the following for permission to reproduce photographs: Alamy p 35 (© AF archive); Corbis pp 7 (Sygma/© Patrick Robert), 22 (politika/© Dung Vo Trung), 29 (Reuters/© Claudia Daut), 34 (epa/© Wang Ying), 40 (© Corbis), 42 (© Bo Zaunders), 44 (Science Faction/© Centers for Disease Control - digital version copyright Science Faction), 47 (epa/© Ricardo Castelan); Getty Images pp 9 (Photographer's Choice/Bruno De Hogues), 12 (PhotoQuest), 15 (Chung Sung-Jun), 16 (Hulton Archive), 26 (IFRC/Japanese Red Cross/Toshirharu Kato), 39 (The Bridgeman Art Library/Spanish School), 45 (AFP Photo/Sonny Tumbelaka); Photoshot pp 30 (WpN/Jeff Topping), 32 (© UPPA), 37 (Xinhua/Rouelle Umali); Reuters p 11 (Nguyen Huy Kham); Shutterstock p 43 (Taras Kolomiyets); The Picture Desk p 49 (The Kobal Collection/Warner Bros./Barry Wetcher).

Design features throughout courtesy of Shutterstock: empty cork memo board, background (© Reinhold Leitner), storm clouds (© KavardakovA), chain link fence (© ARENA Creative). Cover photograph of a man in a protective suit reproduced with permission of Rex Features (Sinopix).

Every effort has been made to contact copyright holders of material reproduced in this book. Any omissions will be rectified in subsequent printings if notice is given to the publisher.

Disclaimer

CONTENTS

Some words are printed in bold, **like this**. You can find out
what they mean by looking in the glossary.

PROLOGUE

In 2017, a super-plague starts unnoticed, but quickly spreads. Unchecked, it could ravage the world.

I don't feel well, Bao. Can you take the geese home?

DAY 1: On a small farm in Dinh To, Vietnam, Hong gets sick...

DAY 5: Tragically, the girl does not recover, and only five days later her funeral is held.

Bao is too sick to come. We pray that he will be better soon.

So many people in the village are sick. What is happening?

DAY 15: A hospital in Hanoi, Vietnam

A nurse and two doctors are sick. And we have 10 more cases from the villages, three of them critical.

This is going to be bad...

It's a virulent strain.

DAY 18: St. Louis, Missouri

FORTY OF THE 186 PEOPLE KNOWN TO HAVE CAUGHT A NEW FORM OF FLU IN VIETNAM AND CAMBODIA HAVE NOW DIED. AIRPORTS AROUND THE WORLD ARE REFUSING TO ACCEPT FLIGHTS FROM HANOI...

Good thing you're safely back home, Wayne.

NEWS   Live

But it takes only one infected person to start a global super-plague. Wayne's family and coworkers have been exposed to the Vietnam flu before he feels sick. People on the plane he flew on, workers in stores he has been to—any of them could have caught it. The crisis has started...

EMERGING SUPER-PLAGUE: DAYS 1-10

When a girl in a remote village in Vietnam gets sick, the family cannot afford a good doctor, and then she dies. It is not an uncommon event. Within days, other family members are getting sick, and then more villagers, but the local doctor can do nothing. After ten days and two deaths, rumors start to spread through social networking sites and local news. Villagers avoid one another, while other people avoid the area. The doctor reports the outbreak and sends four patients to hospitals, but it is too late for them—and for many others.

First signs

A young girl sneezing and coughing attracts little attention. In many parts of the world, the death of a child from a fever is sadly common. Even when Hong's brother gets sick, no one suspects it is a new disease. Many diseases start with common **symptoms**, such as fever, headaches, vomiting, or exhaustion, so it is difficult to spot something new.

The local Vietnamese doctor tries to figure out what is wrong, looking for a known disease. He loses time trying medicines that do not help. Finally, he sends patients to the hospital in Hanoi, where more resources are available to treat people and to **diagnose** the disease. In the hospital, **clinical tests** look for evidence of specific, known illnesses or of the body trying to fight an illness. The doctors correctly suspect the illness is influenza—or the flu—but it is a new, deadly type they have not seen before.

PROFILE OF A PLAGUE

Ebola fever, Zaire, 1976

In August 1976, a horrific disease emerged in the African state of Zaire. Victims developed a high fever, severe headache, vomiting, and dehydration. They then began to bleed from bodily orifices such as the mouth and anus before dying. A disease with such a terrifying symptom soon attracted attention.

The investigation began after a nurse felt sick and was taken to a hospital at Kinshasa. No treatments worked, and she died seven days later. Other health care workers soon died. Blood samples were sent for examination to the Centers for Disease Control in the United States. Scientists discovered the previously unknown Ebola **virus**. Of 318 people who got sick with Ebola fever, 280 died.

TIMELINE: EBOLA FEVER, ZAIRE, 1976

September 1, 1976	First person becomes sick in Yambuku, Zaire
September 16	Dr. Ngoy in Bumba, Zaire, reviews 17 cases; he decides it is an unknown disease
September 21	Sends a message to Kinshasa about **epidemic**
September 23	Experts suspect typhoid fever
September 25	Belgian nurse from Yambuku is moved to Kinshasa for treatment
September 30	Kinshasa hospital is closed; 11 of 17 employees are dead
October 2	Experts collect samples from Kinshasa
October 3	Bumba zone is **quarantined**
October 13	Virus is isolated; it is similar to Marburg virus

Keeping track

The Global Public Health Intelligence Network (GPHIN) is an Internet-based early-warning tool. It constantly searches media sources around the world and in all languages for information about significant new outbreaks of disease. Around 60 percent of outbreak reports picked up by GPHIN come from unofficial sources, including local news, web sites, online discussion groups, and Twitter. GPHIN was developed by Health Canada and the World Health Organization (WHO). Official sources include national governments and health authorities.

Ebola is a deadly and terrifying disease. The bodies of victims are handled with extreme caution.

The investigation starts

Rural Vietnam has few health care resources, and Hong's death is not investigated. But when more people become sick and die and the hospital in Hanoi cannot identify the disease, the investigation begins. Fifteen days after Hong gets sick, the hospital contacts the WHO. Experts from the WHO send tissue samples from patients to leading overseas laboratories: the Centers for Disease Control and Prevention (known as the CDC) in the United States and the European Center for Disease Prevention and Control.

FIRST VICTIM

The first identified victim of a new disease is called the "reference case" or "patient zero." It is not necessarily the first actual case. An epidemic starts where patient zero lived, so the Hanoi flu started in Dinh To.

How diseases work

Every infectious disease is caused by a **pathogen**. The most common pathogens are **bacteria** and viruses.

A bacterium is a small living thing—a microorganism. Bacteria can survive outside the body of the organism (living thing) they infect, called the host. Some can lie dormant for a very long time but spring back into life in the right conditions. Today, bacterial infections can often be treated with **antibiotic** medicines. These kill the bacteria in the patient's body.

Viruses are on the border between living and nonliving things. They comprise a piece of **DNA** or RNA wrapped in a protein coat. Most can survive for only a short time outside a host. They are not affected by antibiotics and need carefully targeted **antiviral medicines** or medicines that boost the patient's **immune** system—the body's own natural way of fighting disease.

Spreading disease

The flu is an airborne disease caused by a virus. When someone who has the flu coughs or sneezes, tiny droplets containing the virus are sprayed into the air. They can fall onto surfaces or be breathed in by other people. If people touch a **contaminated** surface, they can transfer the virus to their hands and then to their eyes or mouth or onto food.

Some diseases are spread through infected body fluids. They do not spread as easily as airborne diseases.

↗

Where people crowd together and touch shared or common objects, disease spreads quickly and easily. In a busy market or shopping center, people come into contact with many others—making an ideal environment for passing on disease.

Other diseases are spread through dirty water or infected food and affect people who swallow the bacteria or virus. These can spread only as far as the supply of contaminated food or water extends.

OUTBREAK, EPIDEMIC, OR PANDEMIC?

- An outbreak of disease happens when more people than usual in an area are affected by a disease. There can be an outbreak of food poisoning, for example, if the food supplied to a large event or school is contaminated.
- An outbreak that affects a lot of people in a population is called an epidemic.
- An outbreak that spreads widely, affecting many people in several countries or the whole world, is a **pandemic**.
- Many diseases are **endemic** in a region or the world. This means that there is always some level of disease. Seasonal flu and colds fall into this category. These are widespread but are not pandemics.

Struggling with the unknown

In Vietnam, people with the unknown disease are taken to hospitals in Hanoi and other cities for better care than they can receive at home. Even there, doctors can only treat the symptoms and try medicines used to treat other viruses, in the hope that they might work. Antibiotics can treat bacterial infections, but a virus such as the flu is harder to treat. Doctors use medicines to lower the patient's fever and give extra oxygen to help the patient to breathe while his or her immune system struggles to fight the disease.

Doctors collect samples from patients for medical researchers to study, both at laboratories in Vietnam and at specialized research institutes abroad. Researchers trying to find the pathogen recognize it is a flu virus, but they discover that it does not match any previously known form of the flu. By day 20, there have been 30 deaths in Vietnam and four cases in Cambodia. The Hanoi flu is spreading quickly, and there is no solution in sight.

What would a super-plague be?

A disease the media might call a "super-plague" would be one that spreads easily from person to person and causes a large number of deaths. It would cause a global pandemic that kills many people. *Super-plague* is not a technical term.

In the past, there have been pandemics of smallpox, cholera, dysentery, measles, polio, yellow fever, bubonic plague (the Black Death), and flu. Few of these could now cause a global pandemic. Dysentery, cholera, and typhoid spread through dirty drinking water, which is usually limited to a small area. Many people are vaccinated against some of these diseases, and smallpox has been wiped out by mass vaccination. Bubonic plague is carried by fleas that live on rodents, which people in developed countries rarely encounter. That leaves the flu as the most likely super-plague. Or, of course, a completely new disease could appear.

Many forms of flu have crossed first from birds or pigs to humans. Human and animal forms of flu are closely related. When a person who is already infected with a human flu virus comes into contact with another form of the flu—either from people or animals—parts of the two viruses can sometimes combine, in a process called **reassortment**, to make a hybrid form with characteristics of both viruses. Hong already had a human flu virus; infection from her birds produced the new form of flu.

A flu can also change by **genetic mutation**. Each time the virus reproduces, there are tiny changes, or errors, in the copying process. These mutations change the features of the flu virus and how it behaves. Some of the changes make the virus less viable, but some give it extra capabilities. A flu from birds could change by mutation to pass between people or (more likely) combine with a human flu virus to create a new type by reassortment.

HOW LIKELY IS IT?

Could we get a flu pandemic from birds?

It is possible that we could get a flu pandemic from birds. The H5N1 flu virus currently circulating in birds in Asia causes serious illness in people. Scientists believe that only three to five specific changes are needed to enable it to spread between people. It could then cause a pandemic. We do not know yet how likely the necessary changes are to happen.

When people spend time in close proximity with infected farm birds, the chance of a flu passing between poultry and people increases.

Super-plagues throughout history

There have been devastating pandemics throughout history. The most famous was the Black Death, which affected Asia, Europe, and Africa in 1346–1351 (see pages 40–41). The Black Death spread more widely than any previous outbreak of disease. More recently, the Spanish flu pandemic of 1918 spread around the whole world.

A plague started by people

A more sinister prospect is that humans could start a plague, either by accidentally releasing a disease from a scientific establishment or by using a disease as a weapon. A super-plague could easily spread from the city attacked to affect a much wider area.

In the movie *I Am Legend* (2007), the world is ravaged by a super-plague that has been created accidentally when a virus intended to cure cancer went wrong and ran out of control (see page 55). This is quite possible; scientists can now create new viruses in a laboratory.

People died so quickly of the flu in 1918 that it was difficult to dispose of the bodies.

PROFILE OF A PLAGUE

Spanish flu (H1N1), 1918

A new type of flu, which became known as the Spanish flu, appeared in Europe at the end of World War I (1914–1918). It was quickly carried around the world by soldiers returning home. Researchers estimate that 50 to 100 million people died.

The first symptoms of the flu were fever and breathing difficulties. Other symptoms included excruciating pain in the head, joints, ears, eyes, and abdomen; partial paralysis; mental disturbances; burst eardrums; and the disintegration of internal organs. Some people bled from the nose—occasionally so vigorously the blood would spurt more than 3 feet (1 meter). It took a long time for doctors to realize that the disease was a flu. There was no effective treatment.

In some cases—particularly in young, healthy people—breathing problems led to pneumonia and death. The disease caused a response called a cytokine storm reaction in the body. The immune system produces chemicals called cytokines to fight disease, but if it produces too many cytokines, the by-products of their action build up to toxic levels. People who died of Spanish flu often drowned in their own blood as their lungs broke down under the assault of the virus and cytokines. Since young, healthy people have stronger immune systems, they produced more cytokines and so were more likely to die.

Terror spread as quickly as the flu. Although many people recovered, some entire families were wiped out overnight. In the village of Brevig, Alaska, only 8 of the 80 inhabitants survived. It is hard to calculate how deadly the disease was worldwide, because only the United States kept reliable records of cases and deaths.

	estimated deaths	1918 population	2012 population	equivalent deaths at 2012 population
United States	675,000	103 million	314 million	2 million
worldwide	50–100 million	1.8 billion	7 billion	194–389 million

STOP THE SPREAD: DAYS 11-33

Health care authorities work to stop the Hanoi flu from spreading by trying to restrict the movement of people who might be infected. But hundreds of people have already come into contact with the victims and have moved to other areas. It is a very challenging task.

How far, how fast?

How quickly a disease spreads depends a lot on the mobility of the people in the affected area. In the Vietnamese village of Dinh To, most people walk or use a bicycle, but they can also travel by bus, and other motor vehicles visit the village and leave again, carrying infected people to other areas of Vietnam. Already, Wayne has carried the virus to the United States and has infected other people on the plane with him, though they are not yet showing symptoms. These people have traveled to other areas of the United States, where they will infect their families and other contacts.

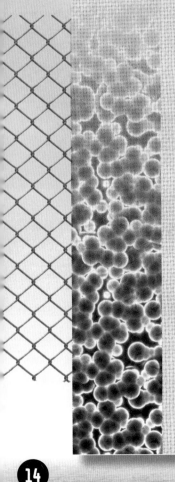

PROFILE OF A PLAGUE

SARS, 2002–2003

In 2002 and 2003, a new disease called SARS (Severe Acute Respiratory Syndrome) was carried around the world in days by air passengers.

SARS is a dangerous respiratory disease characterized by a cough and breathing difficulties. It can lead to pneumonia and death. The reference case was a businessman who traveled from China, through Hong Kong, to Vietnam. Other airplane passengers caught it, and they went on to travel further away. Cases appeared in Canada only two weeks after SARS was first reported in China. Over a few months, the disease reached Asia, Australia, Europe, Africa, and both North and South America. Schools closed in Hong Kong and Singapore.

Fast action to educate the public, trace the contacts of exposed people, and isolate the sick prevented the disease from becoming a pandemic. Even so, there were 8,098 cases, of which 774 people died.

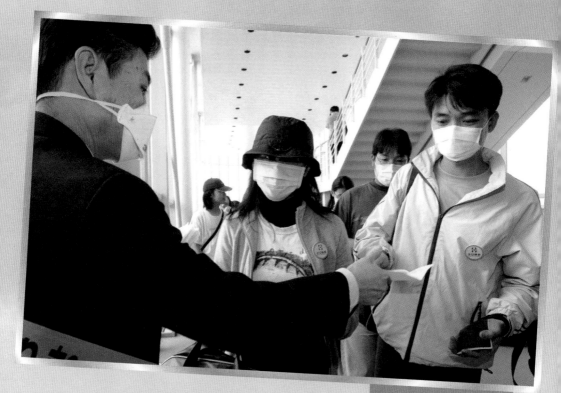

It took five years for the Black Death to spread from Mongolia or northern China to northwest Europe, carried by people traveling on foot or by horse covering no more than 20 miles (32 kilometers) a day. The Spanish flu pandemic of 1918 spread around the world in a few months, carried by soldiers crowded together on ships, buses, and trains.

The Hanoi flu spreads even more quickly, carried by ground and air transportation. The disease can travel halfway around the world in a single day. By day 35, there are cases in the United States, Australia, and Germany as well as Vietnam, Cambodia, Thailand, China, Laos, and Japan. News broadcasts and social media sites spread news of the disease and communicate people's individual experiences of it instantly, leading to widespread panic. Only people in the most remote areas feel safe.

Air travelers in Southeast Asia wear protective face masks as a precaution against SARS in 2003.

Containment and prevention

Medical and government authorities in Vietnam, and later Cambodia and China, work to *contain* the disease (stop it from spreading further) and to *prevent* more people in the area from catching it.

Containing a disease

Hundreds of people try to escape the area around Dinh To. They crowd the buses and drive, cycle, or walk to other villages and towns, going wherever they can. But they carry the disease with them.

In the face of panic, the local authorities quarantine the whole village: no one is allowed to leave. Some still try to escape, running through fields and forests. Everyone in the village is given the antiviral flu medicine Tamiflu. This reduces symptoms, giving people a better chance of recovery and making sick people less infectious.

↗

During outbreaks of the plague in 17th-century Europe, infected houses were closed up with everyone, including healthy people, shut in. This brutal measure condemned many additional people to infection and death.

But it is too late. Infected people have already moved around Vietnam and into Cambodia. Wayne has carried the virus to the United States. The Vietnamese government, taking advice from the WHO, tries to stop people from mixing together. All public gatherings are canceled, and sports stadiums and theaters are closed. China closes its land border with Vietnam, and on day 38, Malaysia refuses to let a plane from Kuala Lumpur to Hanoi land when the pilot radios for medical help upon landing. In Europe and the United States, flights to and from Hanoi are halted immediately.

FACT OR FICTION?

The Plague

Albert Camus's novel *The Plague* (1947) is set during an outbreak of bubonic plague. Here, the Algerian town of Oran has just been quarantined. (Algeria is in northwest Africa.)

"While our townspeople were trying to come to terms with their sudden isolation, the plague was posting sentries at the gates and turning away ships bound for Oran. No vehicle had entered the town since the gates were closed.... The harbor, too, presented a strange appearance to those who looked down on it from the top of the boulevards...gaunt, idle cranes on the wharves, tip-carts lying on their sides, neglected heaps of sacks and barrels—all testified that commerce, too, had died of plague."

Striking a balance

When an epidemic starts, it is impossible to tell how serious it might become. Governments try to balance the risk of damaging trade by preventing travel and closing venues and borders against the risk of allowing a dangerous disease to spread.

Politicians in Vietnam face public pressure to do something. Although they close entertainment venues, they hold off closing schools, colleges, and workplaces until day 25, when the death toll reaches 400.

WHAT WOULD YOU DO?

A big event

If your family had planned a big wedding or other event just as an epidemic of a deadly disease started in a nearby town, what would you want to do? Go ahead with the plans and hope no one infected attends, or disappoint everyone by canceling?

17

Pandemic—it's official

By day 33, it is clear that the outbreak has not been contained. The disease has spread throughout Vietnam, Cambodia, Laos, and southwest China, and there are a few cases in the United States.

People stop traveling to affected areas. Australia, Japan, the United States, and most European countries ban flights to and from Southeast Asia and will not allow ships from Vietnam or Cambodia to dock. Thirty-three days after Hong first felt sick, the WHO declares the Hanoi flu to be a global pandemic.

PANDEMIC ALERT

The WHO monitors disease outbreaks around the world. There are six phases of alert for a flu before a pandemic is declared:

1. No disease circulating in animal populations affects humans.

2. A disease in animal populations has caused illness in humans.

3. An animal or animal–human flu virus has caused small human outbreaks, but it is not generally passing between people.

4. A disease is passing between people, causing local outbreaks.

5. A disease is spreading between people in at least two countries in a WHO region. Mitigation plans should be put into action if they have not already been used.

6. There are outbreaks of disease in at least one country outside the region; a pandemic is underway.

Post-peak period: Infection levels are dropping, but there may still be another wave of disease.

Post-pandemic period: Disease returns to normal, seasonal levels.

Preventing infection

Public information pamphlets, broadcasts, web sites, and text messages give advice, first in Vietnam and then in the rest of Southeast Asia, explaining how people need to take responsibility for their own protection, observing strict hygiene and taking any preventative medicine that is offered. Once the pandemic is official, other countries rush to implement their own pandemic plans and launch public information programs.

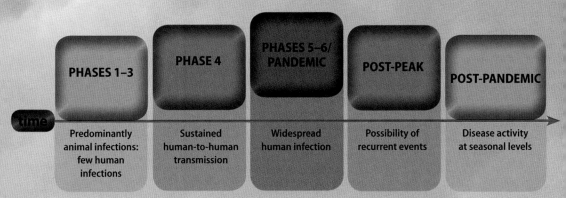

PHASES 1–3	PHASE 4	PHASES 5–6/ PANDEMIC	POST-PEAK	POST-PANDEMIC
Predominantly animal infections: few human infections	Sustained human-to-human transmission	Widespread human infection	Possibility of recurrent events	Disease activity at seasonal levels

Hygiene

An airborne disease can contaminate everyday items such as door handles and ATM machines. Rigorous hand-washing helps to protect people from infection. As public awareness increases, hand-wipes and hand sanitizers start to sell out worldwide.

In hospitals, medical workers are fully covered and use aseptic (completely clean) conditions with no place for viruses or bacteria to lurk. All dressings and medical waste are burned.

These are the phases of pre-pandemic, pandemic, and post-pandemic states, as set out by the World Health Organization.

Public information campaigns stress that the flu can be passed on during the incubation period, when the virus is multiplying in the body but does not yet cause symptoms. People who can afford them wear flu masks all the time; others cover their faces.

As the epidemic worsens, schools, colleges, and nonessential workplaces are shut in Vietnam. People stay at home as much as possible, and the streets and public spaces are empty.

Time lag

It will take weeks to create, test, and approve a **vaccine** and months to manufacture it in large quantities. Before it is available, less specific antiviral medicines offer some protection to infected people.

But these medicines quickly run out. In the United States, Europe, and Australia, people **stockpile** medicines, buying up all or more than they need for their personal use. Manufacturers cannot keep up with demand, and shortages in Southeast Asia—where the medicines are needed immediately—become desperate.

HEALTH CARE UNDER PRESSURE: DAY 34 ONWARD

Health care services in Southeast Asia are stretched to the limit. As cases continue to grow at an alarming rate, there are fears health care might break down completely. Even in countries with few cases, clinics are put under pressure by people who are not sick, but rather simply afraid.

Escalating infection

People fight to get hold of antiviral medicines as soon as they are delivered. In the Far East, where the infection is now raging out of control, frightened people threaten health workers and attack other patients. In China, the army is deployed to protect health clinics and medical workers. Japan issues four million doses of antiviral medicines to health care workers, sparking panic among the population. By day 45, 1,000 people a week are dying in Vietnam, and hospitals can only take some of the most dangerously sick patients. In rural areas, there is no health care available for most sick people.

International medical charities, such as Doctors Without Borders, work alongside the WHO to set up emergency clinics and hospitals in Southeast Asia. But as the disease spreads further, aid agencies can no longer cope.

Investigating the virus

After studying the structure, chemistry, and genome (genetic makeup) of the virus, scientists at the CDC determine that the Hanoi flu is an H5N1 flu variant. This is the same type as the avian flu that has been transmitted between poultry and humans in Southeast Asia since 2003, but it is a new form. They look for similarities with previous strains of flu, in the hope of finding existing medicines that might be effective against it.

Statisticians use figures from hospitals and health care organizations to determine how virulent and dangerous the disease is. First results, after 49 days, suggest the Hanoi flu has an infection rate of 2, meaning each infected person infects another two people. Around 15 percent of those who are infected die. The announcement of the death rate causes global panic.

WHAT WOULD YOU DO?

Medication

Imagine you and your family are well, but your neighbor has become sick with a super-plague. You have medication that you bought in advance; your neighbor has none. Would you give your medication to your neighbor, who needs it immediately, or would you want to keep it in case you or your family needed it later?

PROFILING A PLAGUE

The severity of a pandemic is measured by the case **mortality rate** and the infection rate. The case mortality rate is the proportion of infected people who die. The infection rate (R_0) is the average number of new people infected by each sick person. The infection rate changes over time, as there are fewer people left who have not had the disease.

STAGE 1
Initial $R_0 = 2$

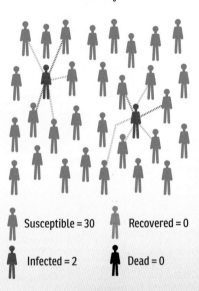

Susceptible = 30   Recovered = 0

Infected = 2   Dead = 0

STAGE 2
$R_0 = 2$

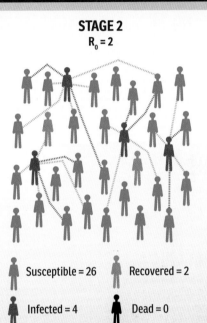

....
contact causes infection

....
contact does not cause infection

Susceptible = 26   Recovered = 2

Infected = 4   Dead = 0

STAGE 3
$R_0 = 1.4$

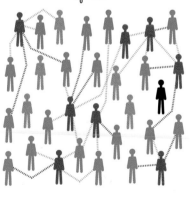

Susceptible = 18   Recovered = 5

Infected = 8   Dead = 1

STAGE 4
$R_0 = 0.4$

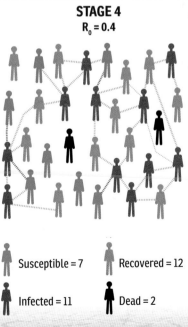

Susceptible = 7   Recovered = 12

Infected = 11   Dead = 2

The number of susceptible people each infected person comes into contact with decreases as a super-plague progresses. Not all contacts are infected.

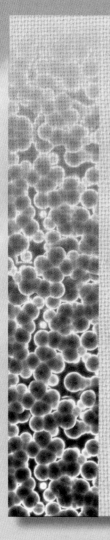

PROFILE OF A PLAGUE

Avian flu (H5N1), 2006–2007

H5N1 is a severe form of flu, commonly called avian or bird flu. The symptoms are fever and shortness of breath, leading to extreme breathing difficulties, then often pneumonia and death. The disease is usually caught directly from birds. During 2006–2007, people around the world feared that H5N1 could become a deadly pandemic.

Supplies of the medicine Tamiflu, which could help with some of the symptoms of the disease, quickly ran low. People in unaffected countries bought the medicine in case they became sick. Some business organizations bought large supplies in the hope of protecting their workforces and preventing disruptions to work. The result was a worldwide shortage of Tamiflu. It became difficult to get supplies to protect people in the Far East, where the disease was spreading—too much had been bought up by people who did not yet need it.

By mid-2012, 606 cases had been confirmed, of which 357 people had died (in total, between 2003 and 2012). This is a case mortality rate of nearly 60 percent. Most cases have been in the Far East and Egypt. (The chart on page 31 shows the case mortalities of this and other diseases.)

↗
Hospitals around the world will quickly come under pressure as medicines and facilities run out.

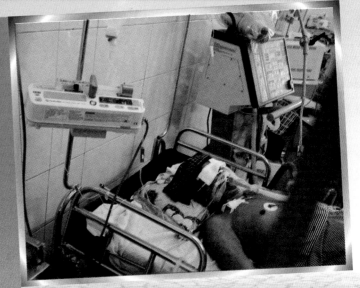

1996	A new strain of flu, H5N1, is found in a goose in China
May 1997	The first human case of H5N1 is found in Hong Kong. Eighteen people catch the flu and six die. All the chickens in Hong Kong are slaughtered to try to prevent the disease from spreading.
February 2003	A family from Hong Kong catches the H5N1 flu after visiting China; three die
December 2003	Three people die of H5N1 in Vietnam
November 2004	The WHO warns that H5N1 could become a pandemic and kill millions; it says in a statement that "much of the world is unprepared for a pandemic"
January 2005	First human-to-human transmission; both people die
February 2005	Vaccines become available for clinical tests
March 2005	The United Kingdom starts to stockpile the antiviral medicine Tamiflu
April 2005	Thousands of waterbirds die from the H5N1 virus at a lake in China
August 2005	The virus spreads far outside China in birds, carried by migrating geese and exported live birds. It reaches Europe in October.
November 2005	The United States launches a $1.7 billion pandemic plan, setting out plans for providing health care, distributing medicines and vaccines, supporting businesses, managing travel, and organizing education
December 2005	Of 143 human cases to date, 76 have died
2006	People outside the Far East begin to die (in Egypt, Turkey, and Iraq). Of 115 new cases this year, 79 die.
Since 2006	Numbers of cases and deaths drop, though not steadily, to around 60 cases a year

The spread of the Hanoi flu

From its start in the village of Dinh To in Vietnam, the deadly Hanoi flu spreads all around the world. Wayne's flight to St. Louis, Missouri, carries it far outside Vietnam and allows the virus to spread from more than one center. It takes only two months to affect nearly every nation on Earth.

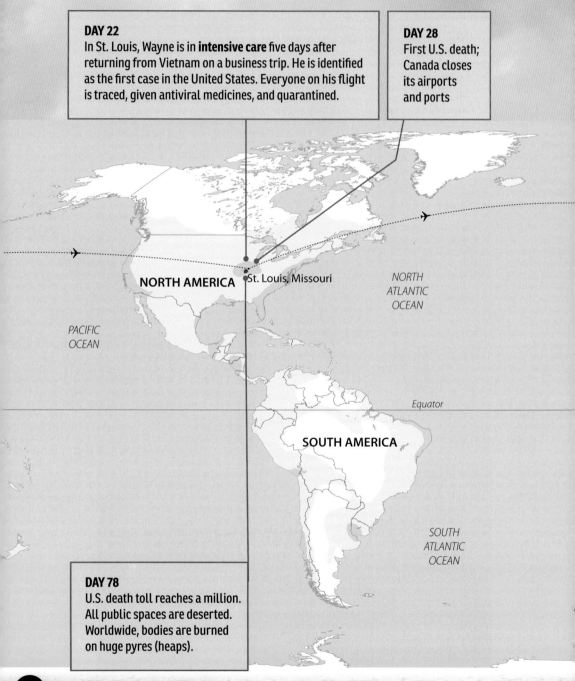

DAY 22
In St. Louis, Wayne is in **intensive care** five days after returning from Vietnam on a business trip. He is identified as the first case in the United States. Everyone on his flight is traced, given antiviral medicines, and quarantined.

DAY 28
First U.S. death; Canada closes its airports and ports

NORTH AMERICA   St. Louis, Missouri

NORTH ATLANTIC OCEAN

PACIFIC OCEAN

Equator

SOUTH AMERICA

SOUTH ATLANTIC OCEAN

DAY 78
U.S. death toll reaches a million. All public spaces are deserted. Worldwide, bodies are burned on huge pyres (heaps).

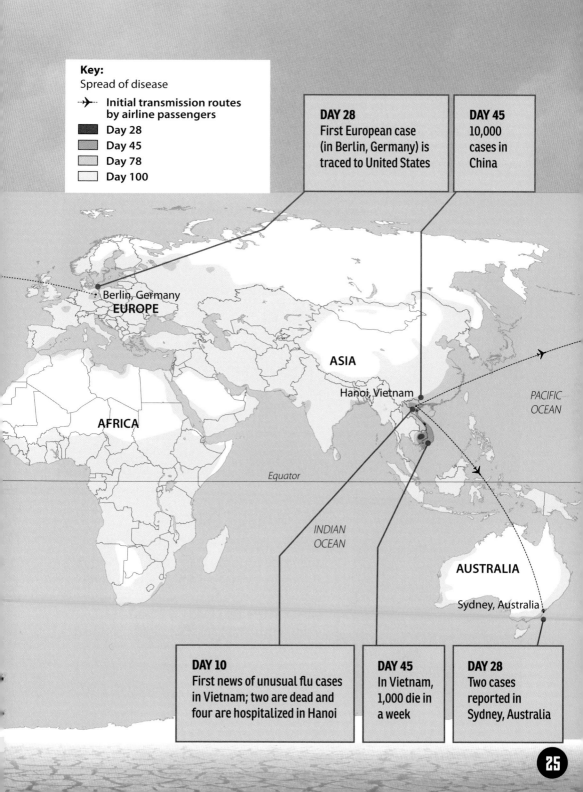

Key:
Spread of disease

✈ Initial transmission routes by airline passengers
Day 28
Day 45
Day 78
Day 100

DAY 28
First European case (in Berlin, Germany) is traced to United States

DAY 45
10,000 cases in China

Berlin, Germany
EUROPE

ASIA

Hanoi, Vietnam

PACIFIC OCEAN

AFRICA

Equator

INDIAN OCEAN

AUSTRALIA

Sydney, Australia

DAY 10
First news of unusual flu cases in Vietnam; two are dead and four are hospitalized in Hanoi

DAY 45
In Vietnam, 1,000 die in a week

DAY 28
Two cases reported in Sydney, Australia

Hospitals at their breaking points

No nation has enough spare health care provisions to cope with a super-plague. The pattern is the same around the world. At first, sick people are taken into hospitals, but the hospitals soon fill up. All routine operations and nonessential care are postponed, and nonemergency cases are no longer being admitted to hospitals. But still, within a few weeks, there are not enough beds, medical supplies, or health care workers to care for all the sick people. The more serious the disease, the more quickly this will happen.

Soon, even people who are dangerously ill cannot go to the hospital, and families have to care for them at home. People die because of a lack of medical care, even in economically developed countries.

In emergency situations, even health care facilities in economically developed countries have to make compromises in care. Here, patients are assessed in the entrance hall of a Red Cross hospital.

Not enough doctors

Medical workers are not immune to illness, and those exposed to patients are very vulnerable. Many become sick, and some die. In some countries, military medical personnel, retired medical experts, and medical students are all brought in to treat the sick, and charity and volunteer workers provide basic care and support.

In 2009, as the "swine flu" spread throughout Mexico (see page 45), the World Bank lent Mexico $205 million. The Mexican authorities used this money to pay for medicine, facilities, planning, and more.

Care in the community

Community care networks are important. During the 1918 flu, some children starved to death because their parents died and no one knew they were alone. Today, cell phones and the Internet will make it possible for people to call for help and for others to check in on people living alone. But some people will be too scared to go near anyone they suspect or know is sick.

FACT OR FICTION?

No hospital beds available

In the novel *Pale Horse, Pale Rider* (1939), Katherine Anne Porter tells the story of Miranda, who is dangerously sick with the flu in 1918. Here, Adam, a friend of Miranda, has tried to find a hospital to take her to.

> There was her door half open, Adam standing with his hand on the knob, and Miss Hobbe with her face all out of shape with terror was crying shrilly,
>
> "I tell you, they must come for her *now*, or I'll put her on the sidewalk...I tell you, this is a plague, a plague, my God, and I've got a houseful of people to think about!"
>
> Adam said, "I know that. They'll come for her tomorrow morning."
>
> "Tomorrow morning, my God, they'd better come now!"
>
> "They can't get an ambulance," said Adam, "and there aren't any beds. And we can't find a doctor or a nurse. They're all busy. That's all there is to it."
>
> "So it's really as bad as that," said Miranda.
>
> "It's as bad as anything can be," said Adam. "All the theaters and nearly all the shops and restaurants are closed, and the streets have been full of funerals all day and ambulances all night..."

LIVING THROUGH IT

As the super-plague spreads quickly around the world, it is like living through a war. People learn to live with fear, to survive with reduced supplies of everything from food to fuel, and to live isolated lives, not traveling or meeting others.

Emergency plans

Most governments have emergency plans for coping during a pandemic. Once it is clear that the Hanoi flu is out of control, nations start putting these plans into action. One nation after another closes ports and airports and then restricts internal travel. But it proves impossible to secure land borders successfully, even using armed guards. In China, guards shoot at people fleeing Vietnam, but many get through at night or in remote areas. In a highly unpopular move, Canada—still free of disease on day 54—closes its border with the United States and announces a shoot-on-sight policy for anyone trying to cross illegally.

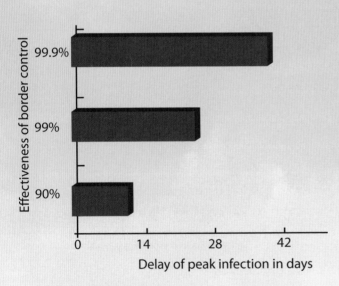

This graph shows that cutting global air travel by 99 percent will delay the peak infection point in countries such as the United States and the United Kingdom by only two to four weeks. It is impossible to stop all air travel— some is essential, and some will continue illegally in private planes.

Life slows down

As the Hanoi flu spreads around the globe, governments everywhere close public venues, including schools and workplaces, to reduce contact between people. Reducing contact slows the spread of disease, which might buy time for a vaccine to be developed. It also cuts pressure on health services, so that more people might be treated.

Many places in Mexico City were closed down during an epidemic of the flu in 2009.

At first, people in unaffected areas do not like having their lives disrupted, but as deaths start in their own countries, they comply with restrictions. Some work or study remotely, with schools and colleges holding classes online. Others have to stop work. Hardship among people with no income leads to a rise in crime in the United States, but it stops quickly after a highly publicized case of a mugger dying when he caught the flu from his victim.

Essential services

National governments struggle to secure food supplies and maintain at least minimal service for water, gas, electricity, fuel, and emergency services while workers are sick. Greece and Peru, then other countries, use soldiers to maintain essential services. But even soldiers are vulnerable, and services break down when there are too few people to run them. In parts of India and the Middle East, breakdown in the water supply leads to widespread shortages and to outbreaks of dysentery and cholera when people are forced to drink contaminated water.

In developed countries, panicked people buy as much food as they can and stockpile it. Stores quickly run out, as they only keep enough supplies for two to seven days. Some introduce **quotas**, and governments use **rationing** for essentials. Vulnerable people, particularly the disabled and elderly, struggle to get the supplies they need.

In cities where the super-plague has become cripplingly severe, essential food supplies are delivered door-to-door by soldiers in armored trucks.

WHAT WOULD YOU DO?

Essential jobs

List five jobs that you think are essential and would still need to be done, no matter how serious a super-plague became. How do you think these jobs could be performed if the people who normally do them were sick or dead?

Running away

Just as people tried to flee Dinh To, many rush to escape as the super-plague reaches their cities or countries. Desperate people undertake dangerous journeys and risk being arrested or shot by guards. But the super-plague is all over the world—there is nowhere to flee and little further risk from people entering a country.

Some people who do escape try to live in remote areas. In the Australian outback and the forests of Russia, Canada, and parts of the United States, thousands of people try to survive in cabins and tents, living on supplies they have brought with them or what they can forage. Hundreds of them die from the flu, accidents, and starvation—and even from being attacked by others who want to steal their supplies. Some survive, but they have a long wait until the pandemic is over and they can return home.

Refugees from towns and cities stricken by the Hanoi flu try to make their way to somewhere safe. Increasingly, this means staying away from strangers altogether.

Dr. Victor Vaughan, acting surgeon general of the U.S. Army, visited an army hospital at Camp Devens, Boston, in September 1918:

> "I saw hundreds of young stalwart men in uniform coming into the wards of the hospital. Every bed was full, yet others crowded in. The faces wore a bluish cast; a cough brought up the blood-stained sputum [spit]. In the morning, the dead bodies are stacked about the morgue like cordwood."

Sixty-three men died the day of his visit.

Victor C. Vaughan, *A Doctor's Memoirs* (Bobbs-Merrill, 1926)

This table shows the death rates of different possible plagues. For all diseases except bubonic plague and H1N1 flu, mortality rates are for people given modern treatments.

Disease	Typical case mortality rate
Seasonal flu	0.008% (1 in 12,500)
H1N1 (1918 Spanish flu)	10–11% (but varying 2.5% to 50% in different populations)
Hanoi flu (as featured in this fictional scenario)	12%
SARS	14–15% (but over 50% in older people)
Small pox (terrorist/ military attack or accident)	30%
H5N1 avian flu	59%
Bubonic plague	Up to 60% without treatment; up to 15% with antibiotics
Ebola fever	90%
Bubonic plague, pneumonic form (see pages 40–41)	100% without treatment

Fear

Once people know the death rate is 12 percent, they start to avoid each other. A disease with a low infection rate but high death rate produces more panic than a disease that infects many and kills few. Some people even abandon sick relatives, terrified that they will catch the flu themselves.

Dealing with the dead

The official figure on day 66 is 250,000 dead—but the real figure is far higher. In areas where large numbers of people live crowded together in poor conditions or are spread out over a wide area, accurately counting cases and deaths is impossible. More than one in every ten people who gets sick dies. But this is not evenly distributed—in some places more people die, and in some places fewer die. By day 78, the official death toll in the United States alone is over a million people.

Graveyards quickly fill up. Dead bodies have to be collected in carts or trucks going through the streets and are buried in mass graves without coffins. Diseased bodies carry the virus, so they must be disposed of quickly. In places where there is no space or workforce to dig, dead bodies are burned.

From bad to worse

In places where people live crowded in poverty, the case mortality rate is as high as 40 percent, and societies become lawless and violent in their panic. In the overcrowded shantytowns of South Africa and Brazil and the slums of India, people begin looting and killing for supplies of food, water, medication, and fuel.

The worst-affected cities and countries declare martial law, in which the army takes control of civil policing and, if necessary, keeps order by force, shooting looters on sight.

HOW LIKELY IS IT?

Will people resort to fake medicines?

It is very likely that people will buy fake medicines. Even in normal times, people with untreatable illnesses sometimes buy fake medicines that will do them no good (and might do harm). During a super-plague, scam artists will take advantage of frightened citizens willing to pay for a cure.

Why catch their Influenza?

YOU need not! Just carry Formamint with you and suck these delicious tablets whenever you are in danger of being infected by other people.

"Suck at least four or five a day"—so says Dr. Hopkirk in his standard work "Influenza"—for "in Formamint we possess the best means of preventing the infective processes which, if neglected, may lead to serious complications."

Seeing that such complications often lead to Pneumonia, Bronchitis, and other dangerous diseases, it is surely worth while to protect yourself by this safe, certain, and inexpensive means. Protect the children, too, for their delicate little organisms are very exposed to germ-attack. Be careful, however, not to confuse Formamint with so-called formalin tablets, but see that it bears the name of the sole manufacturers: Genatosan, Ltd. (British Purchasers of Sanatogen Co.), 12, Chenies Street, London, W.C.1. (Chairman: The Viscountess Rhondda.)

"Attack the germs before they attack you!"

Though genuine Formamint is scarce your chemist can still obtain it for you at the pre-war price—2/3 per bottle. Order it to-day.

Formamint
THE GERM KILLING THROAT TABLET

This advertisement for Formamint tablets promises a preventative measure against the flu epidemic that raged around the world in 1918.

1918

March 11	One soldier at Fort Riley, Kansas, goes to the camp hospital with flu symptoms; by the end of the day, 100 soldiers are sick
July	Public health officials in Philadelphia issue a warning about "Spanish influenza"
August	Sixty sailors in Boston get sick
September	Army hospital beds are filled with flu victims who begin to die. The Massachusetts Department of Health declares an epidemic and warns that it will probably spread to the civilian population.
	Within days of 200,000 people gathering for a public event, 635 new cases of flu are reported. Churches, schools, theaters, and other leisure facilities are ordered to close.
Early October	Parades and sporting events are canceled in Boston. The stock market goes on half-days.
	The epidemic reaches Washington and New Mexico
October 6	In Philadelphia, 289 people die of the flu in one day
Mid-October	In a single day, 851 New Yorkers die. The crime rate in Chicago drops to almost half its usual level.
	In Philadelphia, a vaccine is announced. More than 10,000 complete series of inoculations are prepared, but it is not delivered in time to help.
Late October	**Gauze** masks become compulsory in Washington state
During October	195,000 Americans have died of the flu
November 11	World War I ends. Many people join public celebrations without wearing face masks—cases of flu surge in the following weeks.
November 21	Sirens sound in San Francisco announcing that it is safe for everyone to remove their face masks. (This was a premature decision.)
December	5,000 new cases of influenza are reported in San Francisco

1919

January	Schools reopen in Seattle
March	No flu deaths are reported in Seattle

1919–1920

Winter	Another wave of flu; 11,000 die in New York and Chicago in eight weeks

Vaccination at last

On day 60, scientists in Paris announce they have a vaccine. It is made from a tiny amount of flu virus made safe by heat treatment. It prompts the body to make **antibodies** that protect people if they later encounter the disease.

Usually, new medicines and vaccines are tested extensively before they are used. Now, though, any delay for testing will lead to more infections and deaths—but using an untested vaccine might be dangerous. Some people call for it to be released immediately. It is rushed through testing and released on day 83. There is only enough for 20 million people.

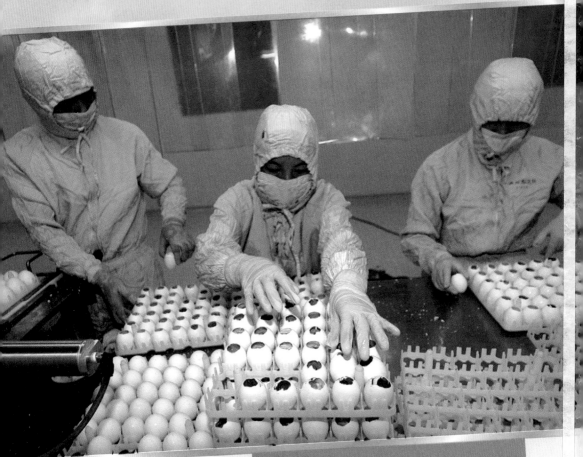

Flu vaccines are produced by growing the virus in chicken eggs, then treating it to make it harmless. It takes 900 million eggs to make 300 million doses of flu vaccine. That could present a serious challenge in a flu pandemic.

HOW LIKELY IS IT?

Total social breakdown

Total social breakdown is possible: many movies and books consider how the world would be if a disaster were so catastrophic that all social order broke down. When food, water, and fuel are in short supply, people often loot, steal, and forage for supplies. However, in the case of a super-plague, people will avoid contact with others, so it is unlikely they will form gangs or riot.

WHAT WOULD YOU DO?

Vaccination

If you had to decide, would you take a vaccine that had not been fully tested or risk catching a super-plague?

"If the [Spanish flu] epidemic continues its mathematical rate of acceleration, civilization could easily disappear… within a matter of a few more weeks."

Victor C. Vaughan, *A Doctor's Memoirs* (Bobbs-Merrill, 1926)

AFTERMATH

No super-plague lasts forever. Eventually, the pandemic subsides. First in Vietnam, where it started, and then elsewhere in the world, the infection rate drops. People wonder how to rebuild their lives.

PANDEMIC WAVES

Many pandemics go in waves, with two, three, or even four waves of disease before they finally stop. Since people who have recovered from a disease are often then immune to it, there are fewer susceptible people to catch and pass on the disease after the first wave. Finally, there are too few for the disease to continue spreading. This happens eventually even if no vaccine or treatment is developed.

Problems for survivors

Some survivors are left disabled or sick even after they have apparently recovered from the Hanoi flu. Some have **postviral** syndromes or breathing difficulties from lung damage. The aftereffects might last for decades: some survivors of the 1918 flu pandemic suffered complications, including mental health problems, that lasted for the rest of their lives.

In addition to people who are still sick or disabled, every country has orphaned children and people suffering the emotional and psychological effects of bereavement and trauma. All around the world, people in poorer societies who need additional care are especially vulnerable.

The first wave of a pandemic often kills the most people. Later waves kill fewer and fewer people, until the disease slips into the background with a low, regular mortality—or disappears completely.

International aid

In the modern world, people of all nations rally to help when others are hit by disaster. International relief efforts provide food, shelter, and medicines to people in need after natural disasters such as floods. But after the super-plague, people in every nation are struggling to survive and feel it is not possible to help strangers in other countries. Even the poorest and hardest-hit nations are thrown back on their own limited resources. Inevitably, many more people die from starvation and illness in the months and years following the super-plague.

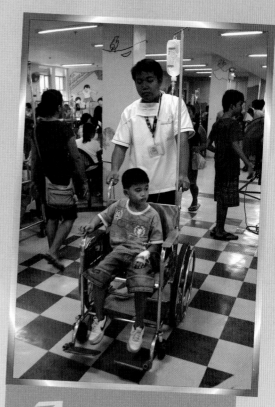

Managed chaos

Life does not return to normal as soon as the super-plague ends. The pandemic has disrupted all aspects of production, including farming, food, medicines, fuel, mining, and manufacturing. There are shortages of many goods, including essentials.

↗ Some people will recover very slowly or incompletely from the super-plague. Will there be sufficient care for them?

Countries that have kept a stable government and adequate law enforcement during the super-plague can deal with extreme shortages. Many societies survive rationing and hardship during wars and natural disasters without falling into **anarchy**. After the Japanese tsunami in 2011, social order was maintained without difficulty. As long as people can see that they are being treated fairly, and everyone has enough to survive, the situation is stable and can improve.

WHAT WOULD YOU DO?

Caring for others

If you survived a super-plague, what would you be willing to do to help people who have been disabled by the disease? Would you take an extra person in your house, share your rations, or do volunteer work? Or do you think caring for unfit people is the responsibility of their families? What if they have no family?

Emergency politics

But elsewhere, extreme conditions lead to upheaval. In lawless areas, in regions where lawgivers and enforcers have died in large numbers and in places where coping strategies have failed, civil unrest follows the super-plague.

People no longer avoid each other. Some form gangs and riot, driven by desperation by the loss of their livelihoods, hunger, and feeling their governments are not acting quickly enough to help them. Some countries that avoided martial law during the pandemic, such as Greece and Ecuador, resort to it now. When there is no time or capacity to deal with issues through the normal channels, martial law provides a brutal way of keeping some form of order.

In some places, governments are overthrown by popular uprisings or by the military taking over to restore order. In other places, dictators emerge, taking over through the violent suppression of other people. Armed gangs emerge and fight for power, seizing land and resources and starting battles and civil wars.

Too few workers

Recovery and rebuilding are slowed down by a reduced workforce. Studies show half the world caught the Hanoi flu, and 12 percent of those people died. That means that 6 percent of the world's population has died.

In 1918, the flu killed 1.3 percent of the healthy young adults in the United States, but around the world, between 5 percent and 10 percent of young adults died. In Samoa, it was around 20 percent. A similar pattern emerges for the Hanoi flu. In the United States and Europe, the death toll is around 8 percent of the population, but in some areas of Africa, India, and South America, it is as high as 30 percent.

HOW LIKELY IS IT?

A return to the Middle Ages

A return to the Middle Ages is unlikely. Apocalyptic movies and novels often show a world after disaster in which society has returned to basic levels of survival, with subsistence farming and no medical care. This is not likely. We have knowledge and technology that we did not have in the Middle Ages. A plague will not damage the physical **infrastructure**, so facilities such as power stations, oil wells, and mines can be up and running again in quite a short time.

In the years after the Black Death, there were not enough farmworkers to farm the land and bring in crops, leading to famine and hardship. The disease killed up to half the population in parts of Europe; farms fell to ruins and lay untended for many years.

It is unlikely we would need to return to medieval methods of survival—it will be easier to find a tractor after a super-plague than oxen and a plow.

Social change

In some places, disaster eventually brings social change for the better. Societies everywhere assess what is important to them and find ways to prioritize those things during recovery. The balance of power changes, and in some places more efficient or effective systems develop. People with essential skills such as medical workers, engineers, and people with basic technical skills are in demand and can easily find work.

After the 1918 flu pandemic, many developed countries put in place public health reforms so that they would be better equipped to deal with a similar emergency in the future. After the Hanoi flu, countries around the globe reassess their health care systems, and some plan improvements.

PROFILE OF A PLAGUE

The Black Death, Europe and Asia, 1346–1350

The plague emerged in Mongolia or China in 1346 and spread slowly through Asia and Europe, carried along trade routes by people on camels or horses and by ship. It was a mixture of bubonic, pneumonic, and septicemic plague, which are three forms of the same disease but are passed on in different ways. The pneumonic form of plague occurs when people breathe in the plague bacteria; it is always fatal. The case mortality rate, depending on the type of plague, was 60 to 100 percent.

The Black Death killed up to 100 million people. In some places, whole villages were wiped out, with everyone dying. The effects were catastrophic. By the time the worst of it was over, half the population of Europe was dead and society was in a state of chaos. There were too few farmworkers to tend the land, raise animals, and bring in crops, so famine and starvation followed the plague. No part of society was untouched, though the poor suffered most. However, in the years after the plague, the surviving workers could demand higher wages and better conditions, leading to big social changes in their favor.

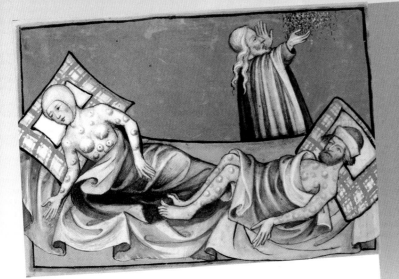

The Black Death had a devastating effect on the survivors. The ravaged countryside and neglected farms led to more hardship and death.

> *"Wretched, terrible, destructive year, the remnants of the people alone remain."*
>
> Inscription at St. Mary's Church, Ashwell, England, 1349

HOW LIKELY IS IT?

Bubonic plague

Another outbreak of the bubonic plague is fairly unlikely: the plague requires contact with rodents that carry infected fleas and can be treated with antibiotics.

However, bubonic plague has been used as a weapon in the past and is a likely choice for a military or terrorist bio-attack. This is the most likely cause of a future plague epidemic.

Rebuilding

In the modern world, a lot of work is mechanized, so the effect of a reduced workforce need not be as devastating as in the past. Major facilities such as power stations and factories are operated by few workers, so some facilities will be easy to operate even with a reduced workforce. Even so, there are still some industries that depend on large numbers of working people, particularly in recently emerging economies such as China and India. The reduced workforce may be a spur to automation or to redistribution of the workforce from nonessential production to essential goods.

Getting things working

A modern economy relies heavily on electrical power, computer networks, and transportation. All industrialized nations rush to restore a full electricity supply and secure fuel deliveries. The United States sends aid and technical workers to Kuwait, Iran, and other oil-producing nations to secure the supply of fuel.

Some of the adaptations and changes people made during the pandemic become permanent. In the United States and Europe, many people continue to work remotely from home and shop online while the fuel supply and public transportation networks are still unreliable. Some see no point in returning to their previous work patterns. Physical items that can be replaced by digital services, such as newspapers, have disappeared in most places. Attempts to restore them fail. The production of unnecessary and luxury items does not restart until economies are confident again, by which time many companies that specialize in them have gone out of business.

Different jobs

Many economies are disrupted, and so is trade. People have to spend their money on essentials, such as food that has become more expensive. Those previously employed in industries that are not essential, such as tourism, entertainment, some financial services, and the arts, are redeployed into essential services. Some people have to take work they do not really want, such as farming or mining, as economies focus on essentials while societies reestablish themselves.

Some tasks are difficult to mechanize, so people have to take jobs they are not used to in order to secure a supply of essentials such as food.

Leftover resources

Unlike a war, a super-plague does not destroy buildings, roads, and airports. It does not pollute water supplies, flood coastal regions, or create deserts. Instead of damage to the infrastructure, the super-plague leaves a surplus in some areas, with spare housing, vehicles, and other goods that people can use.

Although essential consumables such as food, fuel, and medications were used up in the first days of the plague, there has been less demand for clothing, furniture, household goods, tools, and other items that are used up more slowly. Supplies of some of these could last a few years, especially if they are used only as needed and not lost to looters. Surpluses will provide a useful buffer while industries are rebuilt and societies are reorganized.

WHAT WOULD YOU DO?

Prioritizing resources

There are many things we all use every day that are not really necessary. List five products or industries you would get rid of if you had to decide how valuable resources and workers should be used.

REPAIRING THE DAMAGE

All around the world, there is damage that needs to be fixed. In the worst-hit areas, people have to contend with polluted water supplies; dead bodies rotting in public places and rivers; houses, stores, and warehouses that have been looted; and roads that have fallen into disrepair.

During a pandemic, people still get sick with other diseases and still have accidents, become pregnant, and have babies. There are many people who have suffered as a consequence of the super-plague taking all available health care resources, and some now need intensive help.

Fewer people, less pressure
An unexpected effect of the super-plague is that the reductions in manufacturing and transportation are good for the environment. Pressure on scarce or threatened resources, such as water, fuel, and mineral deposits, are eased. Damage to the climate from excess carbon emissions slows down over the period of the pandemic and recovery. One catastrophe could buy us time to help avert a different environmental disaster.

With different priorities, some industries will not recover, but new opportunities will arise, bringing other industries to life. It is impossible to predict how the future will look after a super-plague.

LOOKING TO THE FUTURE

After the super-plague, national and international organizations review how well they handled the situation and try to put in place better plans for a future event of similar proportions.

Studying the disease

It is human instinct to want to wipe out every trace of a super-plague, but medical science progresses by studying diseases and coming to understand how they work, so it is important to collect samples for investigation.

Scientists try to figure out how the super-plague emerged and why it behaved as it did. Careful examination of tissue from people who died from the disease and statistical analysis help scientists to build up a profile of the disease. Statistical studies show who was most and least vulnerable and might give clues as to how the disease works. The high death rate in young adults in 1918, for example, led later investigators to realize that the strong immune systems of young people were actually working against them.

↗

Scientists working on deadly diseases take every precaution possible to prevent the accidental release of a pathogen. This dangerous work helps us to understand and combat disease—but some people think the risk is too great.

WHAT WOULD YOU DO?

Smallpox

Smallpox was wiped out in nature in 1977 and exists now only as samples in Russia and the United States. Some scientists believe it is too dangerous to keep, fearing the virus could be stolen, accidentally released, or used in a war. Others think destroying the last samples that could be used for research would leave the world defenseless. Terrorists could recreate the virus, working from its published genome, and hold the world hostage.

Would you keep or destroy the last two smallpox samples?

PROFILE OF A PLAGUE

Swine flu, 2009

In April 2009, a new form of H1N1 flu from pigs appeared in Mexico. Experts believe it had been circulating for months before being noticed. As it spread rapidly through Mexico, most public and private facilities in Mexico City were closed. Containment failed, and the virus spread around the world.

In June 2009, the WHO stopped counting cases and declared a pandemic. Cases started to decrease in November 2009, and the pandemic was announced to be over in August 2010. Estimates put the death toll at 294,500 people, but possibly as high as 579,000.

The WHO was criticized afterward for spreading panic rather than giving useful information. More than 65 million doses of vaccine were used, but by late 2009, many countries were giving away, returning, or destroying unused vaccines because the pandemic had not been as severe as expected. Reviewing the response to a pandemic should help us to prepare for the next incident.

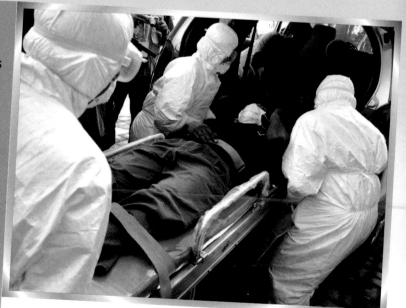

Part of preparedness can be practicing the roles that people will play if a terrible event happens. Emergency services figure out how to deal with incidents such as a terrorist release of a pathogen through these exercises.

Time to recover

The WHO declares that the pandemic is over, but the world cannot relax completely—a second wave could arrive in months.

The vaccine, produced too late to have much impact on the first wave, is produced in large quantities and distributed as quickly as possible. The WHO aims to vaccinate 85 percent of the world's population, hoping to prevent a second wave. Those who have already had the Hanoi flu and recovered from it will be offered the vaccine only after people who have not had it have been vaccinated. This is because survivors have natural immunity that should protect them in a second wave. In reality, the vaccine reaches a large proportion of people only in economically developed countries and urban areas of other countries. But it is enough. A second wave cannot take hold.

The pandemic is over, and the WHO announces that the world is in the post-pandemic period.

As life settles down, the WHO, governments, and health organizations around the world evaluate their response to the super-plague. People analyze what worked and what went wrong. There were many unforeseen consequences, and the pandemic was more widespread and deadly than many plans had made provision for, but lessons learned will feed into new plans.

Remaining alert

We cannot foresee exactly how or where the next super-plague will start, but experts monitor health around the world constantly. It is dangerous to concentrate on only one risk, though. For the last 10 years, scientists have expected that a variant of H5N1 avian flu would be the next pandemic, yet SARS, a previously unknown disease, reached level 5 on the WHO's pandemic alert scale (see page 18).

> *"Criticism is part of an outbreak cycle. We expect and indeed welcome criticism and the chance to discuss it."*
>
> Fadela Chaib, the WHO

The WHO monitors and observes after and between pandemic threats. The objectives of observation are to:

- spot any changes in patterns of flu occurrence or transmission, or the appearance of a new disease
- establish the levels of infection, severity, and impact of disease—unusual patterns can only be identified if we know what the usual pattern is
- identify and monitor the groups who are most vulnerable
- spot any changes in the diseases that are already circulating, including resistance to existing treatments.

HOW LIKELY IS IT?

Another super-plague

Another super-plague is very likely: diseases change all the time. Scientists estimate that a devastating plague like the Black Death occurs only once every thousand years, but a flu pandemic such as that of 1918 will happen every hundred years. However, terrorism, accidents, and warfare might raise the chances of something like the Black Death to 1 in 100 in any particular year. Scientists know it will happen, but not when. It could be next year—or it could be in one thousand years.

Though we are better equipped to deal with a super-plague now than ever before, we are also more vulnerable in many ways.

You can check the current level on the WHO's web site. There is a page for each threat. The page for avian flu, H5N1, is located at the back of this book.

Facing the future

Humankind has always been subject to disease, and another pandemic is inevitable. But with modern planning, preparedness, and advanced medical science, we stand a good chance of limiting the damage. For the first time in human history, we can confront a new disease with an arsenal of knowledge and scientific techniques that give us a good chance of survival.

People who are well informed and prepared are best equipped to survive a super-plague; fear is almost as much of an enemy as disease.

WRITE YOUR OWN STORY

Would you like to write your own story about a super-plague? Here are some questions to ask yourself as you design your plague.

Is your plague caused by a virus or by bacteria?
A bacterial disease can often be tackled with antibiotics, though it might become resistant to the antibiotic used to treat it. With a viral disease, we can often only treat the symptoms and not actually cure the disease.

What are the symptoms?
Many diseases start with common symptoms that don't alert anyone to the seriousness of the illness or signal it as something new. This makes it easy for the disease to get a foothold.

Is there any treatment or a vaccine?
Remember that it can take months to develop, test, and produce large quantities of a treatment or vaccine. If your super-plague spreads and kills quickly, there may be no time to develop these.

How does the disease spread?
Many diseases spread by coughs, sneezes, and personal contact—these spread most easily. But you might find an unusual way to spread the disease in your story.

How deadly is the disease?
Usually, a disease that kills many victims quickly does not cause a serious pandemic, as sick people don't travel or come into contact with many others before they die—unless they live in overcrowded conditions.

In which part of the world did it start?
Diseases are hardest to spot if they start in remote areas—but they also spread more slowly. If a disease is started by a terrorist attack, it will probably hit a large city first.

How did it start? Naturally, or as an act of war or terrorism?
A terrorist attack creates a lot of cases quickly and might be accompanied by other chaos. It could also break out in more than one place at the same time. It could use a known or new disease.

Which measures will governments and international organizations take to try to stop the spread of disease?
These might include stopping the movement of people, closing borders, closing public places, and quarantining sick people and people who have had contact with them.

Destroying infected cities

It is impossible to destroy infected cities. Some movies show the deliberate destruction of a city where a plague has run out of control. This would not happen. It is illegal to kill innocent people and is not in any nation's pandemic contingency plans. In any case, plagues leak out of towns and cities quickly, so even total destruction would not eliminate a super-plague.

Plot and characters

Don't forget that a story needs more than a situation. It needs a plot and characters who readers care about. What will the plot of your story be? How does the plot relate to the plague? It should not just be a story that is set in the time of a plague—the plague should be an essential aspect of the story. Perhaps your main character is trying to find a cure or meet up with a friend or family member shut in (or out of) a quarantined city.

To be exciting, your story must show a character facing difficulties and challenges and finding resources to overcome them. It is much more interesting to read about someone who does something—or tries to do something—than someone who just has things happen to him or her.

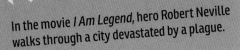

In the movie *I Am Legend*, hero Robert Neville walks through a city devastated by a plague.

TIMELINE

Day 1
A girl gets sick with a severe flu in the village of Dinh To, Vietnam

Day 3
Her brother gets sick

Day 4
The girl dies; six other people are sick

Day 10
First news of unusual flu cases in Vietnam; two are dead, four in hospitals in Hanoi

Day 15
There are 18 cases in hospitals in Hanoi; five people have died. Tests show it is a new form of flu originating in birds.

News of the outbreak spreads quickly through social networking sites and is soon reported by international media as the Hanoi flu

Day 20
Four suspected cases are in Cambodia. There are now 120 cases in Vietnam, with 30 deaths. All chickens and ducks are slaughtered in eastern Vietnam. Governments around the world advise against travel to Vietnam and Cambodia.

Day 22
In St. Louis, Missouri, Wayne is in intensive care five days after returning from Vietnam. He is identified as the first case in the United States. Everyone on his flight is traced, given antiviral medicines, and quarantined.

Three people handling poultry in Vietnam die within four hours of feeling sick. The United States, Europe, Japan, and Australia ban poultry from Vietnam.

Day 25
The WHO issues antiviral drugs to health authorities in Vietnam, Cambodia, Laos, and Thailand. China closes its land borders with Vietnam. The death toll in Vietnam reaches 400. Aid teams struggle to cope.

Day 28
There are 5,000 infected and 540 dead in Vietnam. There is panic in Hanoi as people rush to hospitals and clinics demanding antiviral drugs reserved for medical workers. Chinese border guards shoot three people trying to swim into China by river. Australia, the United States, and most European nations stop incoming flights from affected countries.

Two cases are reported in Sydney, Australia. The first case in Europe is in Berlin, Germany, and is traced to the United States. The first death is reported in the United States. Canada closes its airports and ports.

Day 33
Cases are confirmed in Cambodia, Laos, and southwest China. Four more people get sick in St. Louis, and one dies. Three cases are reported in New York and one in Kansas. Family and known contacts of all victims are given antiviral medicines; immediate family are quarantined.

The WHO declares Hanoi flu a pandemic

Day 38
There are over 20,000 suspected cases in Southeast Asia; clinics in rural areas turn people away. Japan issues 4 million doses of antiviral drugs to health care workers, children, and the elderly.

Day 39
The U.S. government bans travel to Southeast Asia. Australia and Japan close their borders to all but essential traffic.

Day 45
In Vietnam, 1,000 die in a week; there are 10,000 cases in China, 90 dead in Japan, 53 dead in the United States, and 23 in Europe

Day 48
First statistical reports suggest a 10–15 percent mortality, with the highest in people 15–45 years old. A leaked WHO prediction of 250 million deaths creates global panic.

Day 54
Schools and nonessential workplaces close in the United States and Europe. Antiviral medicines sell out and appear on the black market. Canada closes its border with the United States and adopts a shoot-on-sight policy.

Day 60
Japan has 50,000 cases and 4,000 dead; a vaccine is announced and tests begin

Day 62
In China, the death toll passes 30,000; antiviral medicines run out and hospitals close to new cases. Extensive quarantine and travel restrictions take place in all of Asia and southern Russia. Cases worldwide are doubling every three days.

Day 66
More than two million cases are reported worldwide; cases are confirmed in every country. The mortality rate is 12 percent and R_0 is 2.3. Total deaths are 250,000.

Day 78
The U.S. death toll reaches a million. All public spaces are deserted. Worldwide, bodies are burned on huge pyres.

Day 83
A vaccine is approved, but two doses are needed for effective protection; 40 million doses are released

Day 84
A vaccination campaign is announced in the United States. It will take 9 to 12 months to vaccinate everyone. Panic begins as only health care workers are included in first wave of vaccination.

Day 85
A bomb blast in Chicago kills 1,200 in an apartment block; fundamentalist group God's Right Hand claims responsibility, saying it is acting in God's name to further the apocalypse

Day 89
Deaths in China reach 100 million

Day 95
The worldwide death toll is 280 million; the pandemic is slowing in Southeast Asia

Day 110
Numbers of deaths and new cases are dropping around the world

Day 130
In the United States, many businesses and schools reopen

Day 155
The WHO says the Hanoi flu pandemic is over. The death toll is 335 million.

GLOSSARY

anarchy disruption or destruction of social and political order

antibiotic medicine that kills the bacteria that cause disease

antibody protein produced by the body to combat a bacterial or viral disease

antiviral medicine medicine used to treat diseases caused by viruses

bacteria microorganisms, some of which cause disease

clinical test/trial trying out a medicine on human patients to test its safety and effectiveness

contaminate sully (dirty) with material that should not be present

diagnose figure out what is wrong with a sick patient

DNA (deoxyribonucleic acid) complex chemical that carries the genetic code of living organisms

endemic normally present in an area or population

epidemic outbreak of disease with higher levels of infection than usual for that area or population

gauze very thin, flexible fabric

genetic mutation changes that occur to the genetic makeup of an organism when there is a mistake during cell reproduction

immune not susceptible to catching a disease

infrastructure network of roads, railroads, canals, and facilities such as water and electricity supply

intensive care facility providing advanced levels of monitoring and health care for very sick people

mortality rate proportion of people who catch a disease who then die

pandemic outbreak of a disease that spreads over a large area

pathogen organism that can cause a disease, including bacteria, viruses, fungi (a group of simple organisms that includes mushrooms, yeast, and molds) and protozoans (single-celled organisms with some properties similar to animals)

postviral happening after a person has had a viral infection

quarantine period during which infected or possibly infected people are kept separate from uninfected people, originally 40 days

quota allocated quantity

rationing restricting the supply of something by limiting the amount each person may have

reassortment mixing of genetic material between two different viruses to produce a new variant

stockpile buy and store a lot of something, often when it is not immediately needed

symptom change in the body that is the result of an illness, such as headaches or sickness

vaccine small dose of a disease that has been rendered safe and is given to people to prompt immunity to the full disease

virus scrap of genetic material on the edge between living and nonliving things that can cause disease

FIND OUT MORE

Nonfiction

Hardman, Lizabeth. *Plague* (Diseases and Disorders).
   Detroit: Lucent, 2010.

Rooney, Anne. *Infectious Diseases* (Mapping Global Issues).
   Mankato, Minn.: Smart Apple Media, 2012.

Fiction

Camus, Albert. *The Plague*. First published 1947; new edition, New York:
   Thinking, 2011.
An outbreak of bubonic plague in Algeria brings people together in a battle
to survive.

Crichton, Michael. *The Andromeda Strain*. First published 1969; new edition,
   New York: Random House, 2008.
A plague caused by a microbe from outer space threatens humanity.

Web sites

www.cdc.gov/flu
This U.S. Centers for Disease Control web site is full of helpful information
about the flu, with sections about the seasonal flu as well as other types of
flu, such as avian flu and swine flu.

www.who.int/influenza/preparedness/pandemic/h5n1phase/en
The World Health Organization's website where you can see the phases of the
H1N1 virus.

www.flu.gov/pandemic/index.html#
Learn more about how pandemics have spread throughout history and how
pandemic diseases work.

Movies

Contagion (2011, rated PG-13)
Beth Emhoff returns from Hong Kong to the United States with what seems
like a cold. In a few days, she is dead, and other people who have had contact
with her also get sick. The Centers for Disease Control must race to find a
vaccine as more people die.

I Am Legend (2007, rated PG-13)
Robert Neville believes he is the only survivor of a human-made plague that has destroyed humankind, leaving only a few infected mutants. He searches for other survivors, and they battle the mutants, hoping to rebuild society.

Outbreak (1995, rated R)
A deadly hemorrhagic fever emerges in Zaire and is carried to the United States by a smuggled monkey. When a small town in California becomes infected, the U.S. military is engaged to destroy the town and everyone in it.

iPad/iPhone

Plague Inc.
This epidemiology game app allows you to define and develop a pandemic disease and attempt to wipe out humanity with it. A similar free game can be found online at: www.crazymonkeygames.com/Pandemic-2.html.

Topics to research

Here are some topics you might like to research to increase your knowledge about super-plagues or help you write your super-plague story:

- Bioengineering: Scientists can now make entirely new viruses using a tool kit of bits of genetic material. One of the things they make is phages, which are viruses intended to infect and kill bacteria. Investigate how scientists might deliberately introduce new viruses into the body to try to defeat a bacterial illness, and imagine how this could go wrong.

- Plagues in other organisms: Humans are not the only organisms that can suffer from a super-plague. A disease that destroyed all wheat, all rice, all bees, or even all grass would have just as devastating an effect on people as a human super-plague. It might even be worse. Find out how disruption of food chains and food webs by disease could harm humanity.

INDEX